CONTENTS

Title Page	1
Bulgaria as a travel destination	3
How to get to Bulgaria	5
You can travel to Bulgaria in different ways	6
Which airline to choose?	8
Another way to travel to Bulgaria is by car	12
What documents will you need when travelling by car?	14
There are some tips related to your driving:	20
People with more adventurous spirits can chose to travel to Bulgaria by bus	22
Have you ever considered a shared travel by car to Bulgaria?	24
How to travel in Bulgaria	26
Where and what to eat on holiday in Bulgaria?	29
Stray cats and dogs	32
Mosquitoes and other insects	34
Medical help and first aid	36
Climate conditions	37
Currency exchange	38
How to book accommodation?	39
Places to stay when on holiday in Bulgaria	42
Enjoy your journey to Bulgaria	49

TRAVEL TO BULGARIA FROM GREAT BRITAIN

FOR INDEPENDENT TOURISTS

by ALEX HUNTER

BULGARIA AS A TRAVEL DESTINATION

Over the years Bulgaria has become one of the preferred holiday destinations for British tourists. Perhaps you have already spent a summer or winter holiday there, or you know people at work or in your neighborhood who have just come back from the sunny beaches or snowy mountains of Bulgaria. You can see various offers for package holidays in Bulgaria and the costs vary from 350 to 750 pounds per week per person. Bulgaria is a relatively cheap destination and one of the favorite holiday places for big companies as like as the recently bankrupted Thomas Cook. The package holidays are easy to buy and safe, however, you will be tempted to spend the whole week in the all-inclusive hotel. There is nothing wrong to just lie under the sun, beside the swimming-pool and eat and drink as much as possible. However, if you have already spent a holiday like this, or if you like doing more interesting things rather than baking in the sun, you may be attracted by the idea to discover Bulgaria by yourself, in your own pace, visiting places of interest and getting out of the routine. I am going to do my best to provide as much information as possible for those adventurers who may want to experience something different, not included in the all-inclusive holiday packages. Being a traveler for many years, I have been independently discovering the beauty of the world. It is always

Alex Hunter

worthy to get out of the crowd and to taste the new place. Now, get ready for adventures!

HOW TO GET TO BULGARIA

Bulgaria is situated in the South-eastern part of Europe; its neighbors are Greece and Turkey to the South, Romania to the North, Serbia and Macedonia to the west and Black Sea to the East. It is a relatively small country, with population about 6 million people. Despite its small size, Bulgaria is rich of mountains, rivers, lakes, and a long coastal line. The climate conditions in summer make it a preferred place for tourists. In fact, summer temperatures along the sea coast do not fall below 22°C which makes it perfect for sunbathing. Winters can be freezing, with temperatures below -15°C, however, after a whole day in the snow tourists will be able to warm themselves in front of the fireplaces in the hotels, with a cup of good tea or a glass of good alcoholic drink. Bulgaria is famous for its beaches in summer and ski resorts in winter.

❖ ❖ ❖

Alex Hunter

YOU CAN TRAVEL TO BULGARIA IN DIFFERENT WAYS

The fastest and easiest way to reach your destination is by airplane. Many companies fly to Bulgarian capital Sofia, as well as to both major seaside towns- Bourgas and Varna /only in summer season, between May and October/ and one low-cost company /Ryanair/ flies to Plovdiv, which is the second Bulgarian town in terms of population and the gate to the beautiful Rhodope mountain and the famous ski resorts. Low budget companies usually offer good prices for return flights. If you plan your summer holiday before the middle of July, you can easily get good offers. Please, if possible, avoid flying between July 15 and the end of August- otherwise you will get ripped off your savings. The flight prices jump as crazy a week before the school summer holiday starts. For example, in the beginning of July you will be able to find a one-way ticket to Sofia for the price of about 80 pounds or less /return for less than 150/. The same ticket will cost you more than 200 pounds in one direction from the middle of July. Of course, August is the craziest month to fly and from beginning of September prices go down. Even if you have children at school, it can be cheaper to pay the council fines and to take them to holiday before the official end of school year. Moreover, kids would benefit from an experience abroad, would get the chance to learn about history, geography, culture of a new country and, possibly, to learn some foreign words. Travel is always beneficial for young minds, they are curious by nature and a holiday abroad would enrich their perception of the world.

Remember, whenever kids have school breaks, prices of flights jump.

Alternatively, if you buy a holiday package from a tourist company like the recently bankrupted Thomas Cook or TUI, you will be provided with charter flights to your place of destination, therefore, you will not need to worry about flight prices- they will be included in the package price. However, if you want to experience more, to see more and to taste more, it is recommendable to avoid buying all-inclusive packs and to tailor make your own unforgettable holiday.

WHICH AIRLINE TO CHOOSE?

First, it depends on the location where you live. It is always easier to choose the closest airport to fly from and then to search for airlines. However, there are some tips to be taken into consideration:

- There are airlines which are not very reliable. For example, I would always avoid using Ryanair because they have proven themselves as a company you cannot rely on. Their tickets are probably the cheapest but you can never know whether the plane will take off or the flight will be cancel. It is like gambling- if you are a devoted gambler and not in a rush, you can try to fly with them- at least you will get cheap tickets. Thus, it would be worthy to do some research and see which airline has had recent problems with flights. The research will help you to avoid some disappointments and, most probably, will guarantee you a hassle free start of your holiday.

- Some of the airlines have invented ridiculous restrictions on luggage. You should carefully check the size of hand luggage allowed on board and the prices for the checked-in luggage. Sometimes the luggage can cost more than the ticket; therefore the use of that particular airline would be senseless. If you head to Bulgaria for a summer holiday, you can carry only hand luggage. Usually weather in summer is nice and warm, with no rain or strong winds. The temperatures range from 25°C up to 40°C. You will not need to put in your luggage lots of warm clothes or shoes. A waterproof jacket will be enough to protect you in case of a sudden drop in temperatures. Therefore, you can just fill in one small suitcase or a backpack, put the jacket on and beat the stupid prices for the additional bags. The size allowed for the hand luggage varies for different airlines. Wizz Air and Ryanair have recently restricted the size again to just one small bag / much smaller than the allowance of Easy Jet /. Check the size allowed on the airline website before buying the suitcase.

- You can choose your airline depending on the place of your holiday. However, in some cases, especially if you intend to rent a car, it can be much cheaper to fly to the capital city and then to travel by car to your destination. You just need to do some research and comparison of prices. Use Skyscanner /www.skyscanner.net / to find some good offers for flight tickets, car hire, etc. There are web sites as like as www.kayak.co.uk or www.booking.com which will show you some good offers for car rental. You can also always have a look at the web sites of the airlines or rent-a-car companies. Sometimes there can be a slight difference between the comparison sites and the companies' own web sites. As a tip, I can say that the fuel you will need to drive from Sofia to the seaside would cost you about 100 pounds /on average, depending on the type of car/.

- Food and drinks on board of the low budget airlines are not for free, they will cost on average 6-7 pounds per person. There are airlines as like as Bulgaria Air or British Airways which include the food, drinks and 20kg luggage allowance in the price of the ticket. However, their tickets are more expensive and sometimes the airport their flying from, is not the most convenient for the holiday makers.

- In general, I would advise you to have a look at the main airlines which fly to Bulgaria- Easy Jet, Wizz Air, Ryanair /although I would not recommend this one/, Bulgarian Air and British Airways, to check the prices, the airports, to do the calculations and to buy the tickets. Alternatively, you can use the comparison sites as like as Skyscanner to find the best offers.

If you fly to Sofia with a low-cost airline, you will arrive at Terminal 1, the old terminal, which would be a bit of a shock for you. It is far from the big UK or European airports and resembles a village bus station. The good thing is that the cue for the passport control goes quite fast and you would not be required to wait for a long time to get your passports checked. There are only two belts for the luggage; therefore, you can promptly orientate where to look for your bags.

When you go out, try to avoid the illegal taxi drivers who will be waiting for tourists to come. If you take an illegal taxi, it can cost you too much. The illegal taxi drivers are hunting for foreign tourists at the exit of the terminal, offering to help with luggage. They can be very polite and helpful but they see you only as an ATM. Taking an illegal taxi usually will cost you three times the normal price. Thus, ask for the prices first. A taxi from the airport to the city center should not cost, in any case, more than 16 Bulgarian leva /about 8 pounds/. If you cannot find a normal taxi, take the free shuttle bus to Terminal 2 /every 20 minutes/ and then take the underground /only 1 pound per person/.

If you fly to Plovdiv, instead of Sofia, your only solution will be to take a taxi from the airport to the center. Unfortunately, at the moment there no public transport goes to the Plovdiv airport. The same is the situation with Varna airport- you should either rent a car from the terminal, or rely on taxis to go to the town center.

On the reverse, the airport of Bourgas does have a reliable connection to the town center via public transport. You can take bus number 15 /every 20 minutes/ from the bus stop at the terminal. It will cost only 0.50 pounds per person. Of course, there are also taxis; however, the price of the legitimate taxis should not exceed 16-17 Bulgarian leva.

Avoid exchanging currency at the airport terminals- the rate is much worse than the normal exchange rate. You possibly will end with less money than expected if you use the currency exchange facilities at the airports. A good tip here will be checking the official rate first.

Alex Hunter

ANOTHER WAY TO TRAVEL TO BULGARIA IS BY CAR

It can be real fun if you have the option for a longer summer holiday and if you travel with children. Travelling by your own car will automatically spare you worries related to luggage allowances, food, drink, airports, car rentals, taxi drivers, etc. Kids will definitely benefit from such experience. As I mentioned above, they are curious by nature. Following the map, talking to different people, visiting interesting places while travelling will broaden their knowledge and skills. They would pick some foreign words, or, if they study languages at school, they can put their skills in practice. However, it is a long route to drive and the driver should be prepared to stop at various places, to have some rest, to allow children to stretch and walk around. If you decide to drive to Bulgaria, you need to calculate at least 2.5 days in one direction. Of course, if you intend to travel without children, you can reach your final destination in less than 24 hours- in that case you will need to have at least one additional driver to change.

When you travel with kids, you need to consider at least one night in a hotel or motel /most probably in Germany or Austria, depending on the time you leave UK in the morning/. Hotels and motels along the road are not very expensive, a room in Germany costs about 60 pounds, in Austria can be about 90-100 pounds / prices are per rooms, not per person/. It would be better to foresee two overnights at hotels before reaching Bulgarian border. If you stay first night in Germany, the second night can be in a hotel in Hungary or even in Romania. You can book the hotel stay in advance but if you would not like to be restricted in time or pushed to drive beyond your abilities, I would recommend to just search for a random hotel along your route.

WHAT DOCUMENTS WILL YOU NEED WHEN TRAVELLING BY CAR?

- Driving licence: You can still drive in Bulgaria, as well as in the European Union with your UK driving licence /if the UK leaves the European Union, you will need to get an International Driving Permit /IDP/. The International Driving Permit can be purchased from the Post offices as a supplement to the UK licence. You can check the government website: www.gov.uk for the most-up-to-date information. An International Driving Permit will cost /most probably/ 11 pounds for travelling in multiple countries.
- Green Card: in event of Brexit you will be advised to buy additional insurance cover- the so-called Green Card. Green Cards are an international certificate of insurance issued by insurance providers in the UK, guaranteeing that the motorist has the necessary third-party motor insurance cover for travel in the particular country. They are not cards but paper documents which under current international rules, should be printed on green paper. Motorists should contact their vehicle insurers to obtain a green card both for their car and, if they are towing, for their trailer or caravan as well. There may be an administrative cost involved.
- If you intend to travel with your pet, you should firstly check the advice published by the Government in November 2018 for those seeking to take their pets away with them

on their European trip:
1. You must have your dog or cat microchipped and vaccinated against rabies before it can travel. Your pet must have a blood sample taken at least 30 days after its last rabies vaccination. Your vet may recommend a booster rabies vaccination before this test.
2. Your vet must send the blood sample to an EU-approved blood testing laboratory.
3. The results of the blood test must show that the vaccination was successful.
4. You must wait three months from the date the successful blood sample was taken before you travel.
5. You must take your pet to a Official Veterinarian no more than 10 days before travel to get a health certificate.

- Car stickers: In case of Brexit, UK-registered cars will need to display a GB sticker when driving in any of the 27 EU countries.
- MOT certificate- you should have a valid certificate stating that your car has successfully passed MOT. Although there are no borders between the countries in Schengen zone, you will be asked to show the MOT certificate to the border authorities at Hungarian-Romanian border and, probably, at the border between Romania and Bulgaria, too.
- You need to carefully plan your travel. Open the map and decide where would be the best place to leave the UK borders and to enter the European mainland. I would advise you to avoid passing Calais in France. Although Dover-Calais is, probably, the most popular route with convenient ferries, etc., there are too many issues with migrants and Calais. If you want to use Dover port, the better option is to take the ferry to Dunkerque. You would avoid crowds at Calais, possible problems there and have a safer start of your adventure. Due to same reasons, please, avoid the Eurotunnel-

there have been too many problems with migrants trying to board random cars, etc. Moreover, you will avoid endless cues by choosing Dunkerque. DFDS is the ferry company which carries cars and passengers from Dover to France. You can visit their web site: www.dfdsseaways.co.uk. You can also have a look at: www.aferry.co.uk, or just search in Google to compare prices and timetables. If you choose to get a ferry in the morning or before lunch time, most probably you will be able to pass France, Belgium and the Netherlands before night and to stop for a rest and sleep in Germany. It is real fun to just drive without need to pass any borders and customs control at all. You would just look at the signs along the road saying: Welcome to Netherlands, Welcome to Belgium, or Welcome to Germany. You would detect some changes in the architecture, in roads, petrol stations, etc. in my opinion /from my own experience/, the most difficult petrol stations are in France. As I do not speak much of French it was not very easy to understand how exactly we were supposed to put fuel in the car. In fact, it appeared that you need to go to the counter and to say how much fuel you want to put. You should pay in advance and then will be able to fuel the car. Well, we spent long time in the night at our first French petrol station to try to guess what to do.

- In general, in the other countries on your route the petrol stations are easier to use. There are usually restaurants or places where you can buy some food at the petrol stations. The best thing when you travel by car is that you can take whatever food or drinks you would like with you. Therefore, if you have got a favorite food or drink, you will not need to worry whether you would find it abroad or not. You can just put it in the car.

- Instead of Dover-Dunkerque ferry, you may choose to take the ferry from Newhaven to Dieppe. It is pretty convenient for people who live in East or west Sussex. The ferry trip takes longer time than the Dover-Dunkerque and you will need to make a longer trip through France. However, it would not be necessary to pass Netherlands or Belgium because you will enter Germany directly from France. Technically, this is the shortest route if you live in Sussex or the Western part of UK according to the satellite navigation. Try to avoid French highways and take the secondary roads- you will save much of money for toll fees and will be able to enjoy the beautiful French towns and villages, as well as to taste the delicious French food.

If you live up in the North, you can skip passing France by taking the ferry from Newcastle to Amsterdam /see www.dfdsseaways.co.uk for details/. It is an overnight trip, thus you will have the advantage to sleep during the sea crossing. In the morning /at about 10 a.m./ you will be able to start your driving adventure full of strength and enthusiasm after a good overnight rest.

Another option can be the ferry from Hull to Belgium or the Netherlands /it goes to Zeebrugge in Belgium and Rotterdam in the Netherlands, see www.poferries.com /. Both are overnight sailings and you will have the chance to start your European journey after a good sleep onboard.
In general, I do like ferries- they are comfortable, food is good and not much overpriced and kids can entertain in some of the many kids' corners.

When traveling by car you will need to usually pass France, Belgium, a tiny part of the Netherlands, Germany /prepare for a long drive in Germany, it is a large country/, Austria, Hungary, Romania /long drive as well/ and you will reach Bulgarian border. Alternatively, you can chose to drive through a big part of France, heading to the south, after that to pass Germany, Austria, Hungary and Romania again. An alternative and a very spectacular route, but also a longer one, will be if you enter Italy from France, drive across Northern Italy and then pass Slovenia /a very beautiful country, especially at night- it is like a fairy tale/, Croatia, Serbia and Bulgaria. The problem here would be the Serbian border. As this country is still not an EU-member, most probably there would be massive cues at the border checkpoints and customs in both directions- when you enter and when you leave the country. Luckily, there is a way to avoid passing Serbia- by entering Hungary from Croatia, then passing Romania and entering Bulgaria. If you chose the scenic route through Italy, Slovenia, and Croatia, you will need to calculate one extra day for your journey.

In general, European roads are in good condition. As I mentioned above, try to avoid highways in France because there are fees and you would have to stop many times to pay highway fees, which could be very irritating. If you chose the secondary French roads, you will be able to see many towns and villages, to stop somewhere to eat and relax, to visit some places of interest, etc. There are no fees for highways in Germany, Belgium or Holland. On entering Austria, you need to buy a vignette at the first petrol station after passing the border sign. Otherwise you risk a fine. In Hungary, Romania and Bulgaria you need to buy vignettes as well. It is possible to buy the Hungarian vignette before crossing the border coming from Austria. The first border control you would see during your journey after leaving the UK would be at the border between Hungary and Romania. You will leave the Schengen zone by crossing that border; therefore, the Hungarian customs officers can be very strict. They will thoroughly check your ID documents, the documents of the car, the MOT certificate, the documents of your pets /if any/. There would possibly be a cue of cars at the border so it would be a good place to stretch and to relax for a while. If you had no overnight rest in Austria or Hungary, it would be most recommendable to find a hotel or motel in Romania. Do not drive if you are tired, it would not be safe and could put your life and the life of your family in danger. Hotels in Romania are usually in a good condition, relatively cheap and clean.

You have got two alternative routes to go to Bulgaria through Romania: you can either use the Danube Bridge from Calafat to Vidin /6 Euro fee per car/- check http://www.vidincalafatbridge.bg, or the Danube Bridge from Giurgiu to Ruse /2 Euro fee per car/. If you are heading to Bulgarian seaside resorts, it is better to pass through whole Romania /following the highway to Bucharest/ and cross the Danube Bridge from Giurgiu to Ruse. Thus, you will pass Bulgarian border not very far from the seaside and after one or two hours drive you will be able to check in your hotel. If you are heading to the mountain resorts or winter ski resorts, the better crossing place would be the Danube Bridge between Calafat and Vidin /follow the highway to Cluj-Napoca, then the road to Giurgiu/. Thus, you would be able to head directly to your destination, without passing the whole Romanian territory. There would be border checks between Romania and Bulgaria again. However, they would not be as strict as at the Hungarian border because you are not entering a Schengen country.

THERE ARE SOME TIPS RELATED TO YOUR DRIVING:

- 	Please, do not forget that in Europe you should drive on the opposite side of the road, therefore you have to drive on the right. If you have no experience with driving on the right side, give yourself extra time to get to your destination and take regular breaks. You should be very careful when overtaking and at roundabouts and junctions.
- 	If you're taking your own vehicle abroad, you'll need headlight converters. That's because at night the headlights of cars designed for driving on the left-hand side of the road will dazzle oncoming drivers in countries where you drive on the right. It's a legal requirement in most European countries not to dazzle oncoming drivers.
- 	If you travel with kids, you will need car seats for them in Europe. Children under 10kg must sit in special car seats, especially designed for babies. Children between the weights of 9 and 18kg must use a suitable car seat. Those between 15 and 36kg must be sat on a booster seat or car seat using an adult belt. Children under 13 years are not allowed to sit in the front of the car.
- 	Roads along your route will, in general, be in a good condition. However, you must drive more carefully in Bulgaria. Although many roads were recently repaired and improved, there are still lots of potholes on the roads. Avoid entering

the potholes, if possible, otherwise you can break your vehicle /you can never know how deep is the pothole/. You would not really want to spend your holiday repairing your car.

- Always observe speed limits. You would not really like to receive a huge fine while driving or to participate in a car accident. Speed limits can differ in different countries.

- Exchange currency before starting your journey. Most credit and debit cards are accepted in Europe; however, you would not want to find yourself at a fuel station with a broken ATM machine and POS terminal, without any cash in your pocket, in the middle of nowhere. Cash is always useful. Euro /EUR/ is the currency in France, Netherlands, Belgium, Germany, Italy, Slovenia and Austria. You will need Hungarian forints /HUF/ for Hungary and Romanian leus /RON/ for Romania. If you are driving through Croatia and Serbia, you will need Croatian kunas /HRK/ and Serbian dinars /RSD/, respectively. On entering Bulgaria you will need cash in Bulgarian leva /BGN/. Although some shops would accept payments in Euro, it will be much cheaper and easier for you, if you have got some cash in local currency. Usually, if you try to pay in Euro in the shops, the exchange rate will be much higher than normal.

The costs for travelling by car could be higher than the costs for plane tickets. Depending on the type of the car, you would, probably, need at least 500 pounds for fuel and overnight stays in one direction. However, you will save some extra money because you will not need to rent a car in Bulgaria. Moreover, a car journey can be very educative for children and can boost their imagination and desire to learn.

PEOPLE WITH MORE ADVENTUROUS SPIRITS CAN CHOSE TO TRAVEL TO BULGARIA BY BUS

Many bus companies travel once or twice a week. There are some pros and cons related to this option. The bus tickets are relatively cheap; they do not change prices during school holidays or other high periods. You are allowed to take much more luggage for free in the bus which can be very useful if you intend to spend more time on holiday. You can take your ski equipment, bike, or surf for free. You are also allowed to take food and drinks in your luggage, thus you will not worry where and when to eat. If you do not like planes, want to take more luggage with you, travel during the school holidays or festive periods, do not want to drive, bus would be the ideal option for you. You have to consider that, unlike travelling by car, when you travel by bus, you will not stay overnight in hotels. It can be exhausting if you are not used to sleep in a vehicle. Although the bus will stop every 3 or 4 hours for rest and use of toilets, you need to be prepared that your legs will hurt at the end of the journey. You cannot do much to avoid swollen legs and ankles. You need to have flip-flops or slippers for the bus, to avoid putting too much pressure on your feet. Whenever the bus stops, you need to go outside and walk around, to relieve your feet. The bus travel lasts about 2 days and nights; therefore you should be prepared for some inconvenience during the journey. Do not forget to take a light blanket with you- it can become very cold during the night in the bus. It is not always easy to get asleep on the bus, with people around and lights on. However, if you are young in spirit, do not mind some inconveniences, love adventures and would like to see European routes without driving, bus can be your favorite means of transport. To sum up: it is relatively cheap /about 200 pounds for return ticket/, reliable, someone else will drive, and you can take much of luggage and equipment with you. Of course, it is not suitable to travel with children- they will need more rest and overnight sleep.

You can check and compare buses at: www.busradar.bg. Alternatively, you can check Google. Just write: buses from UK to Bulgaria and you will get the results.

Alex Hunter

HAVE YOU EVER CONSIDERED A SHARED TRAVEL BY CAR TO BULGARIA?

This is another option, which is also cheap and fast. You can usually find adverts related to share travelling by car in social media. Drivers are preferred because you would participate in driving at some point. The aim is to travel as fast as possible, usually under 24 hours. In most occasions you will be required to pay about 100 pounds in one direction if you help with driving. Same as the bus travel, shared travel is not suitable for families with children. It would be suitable for you if you are a driver, want to get fast to your final point, want to carry much of luggage, and prefer to travel by road, not by air. Sometimes you can even find offers for a driver to drive a car to Bulgaria without paying anything. In fact, you will receive a free car journey in return for your driving skills- not a bad deal at all. Again, you can find offers like this in the social media or Google. There are lots of groups in Facebook, for example, created for Bulgarians abroad, which advertise shared journeys by car. Usually, the people who place ads related to the shared car travels, are able to communicate in good English, so do not hesitate to contact them if you would like to use that cheap option.

Alex Hunter

HOW TO TRAVEL IN BULGARIA

There are several options to choose from if you want to go from point A to point B in Bulgaria.

In case you have rented a car, you can drive it almost everywhere on the roads. Be careful, there are some roads marked on the maps, which in fact would not exist. They have been planned in the past, put on the maps; however, they have never been built. Those phantom roads could get you stuck in the middle of nowhere. In general, the satellite navigation will not deceive you but you need to carefully watch the road.

If you arrive in Sofia and need to go to the seaside, there are two main highways which will take you to the Northern sea coast or to the Southern sea coast. The highway named "Hemus" will take you from Sofia to the town of Varna. That journey would ideally last about 4.30 hours. In the peak seasons there can be traffic jams at some places and the driving would take longer time. The southern highway is named "Thracia" and will take you to the town of Bourgas and the south coast. Again, journey would roughly last about 4.30 hours, depending on the traffic and road conditions. Both highways are relatively new, however, every year there are repair works in parts of them. Please, remember that on the highways there are not many places to stop for food, so better get some snacks and drinks with you in the car.

You can choose to travel by bus. Bus journey takes longer- between 6 and 7 hours, the price is 15-16 pounds per person in one direction. The advantage of the bus is that you will not drive and will not get tired. There are overnight buses as well and you can, possibly, sleep while travelling. Buses also stop at designated points for food and drink, as well as for toilet use. Most of the buses are comfortable enough, however, some of them can break down during the journey. My advice here will be: avoid the company named "Union-Ivkoni", most of the accidental bus breakdowns have happened with its buses, which are old and unreliable. Check the buses and timetables at: www.centralnaavtogara.bg.

For people with more adventurous attitude I would recommend to take the train from Sofia /Central station/ to Varna or Bourgas. Bulgarian trains usually run on time, there are no sudden train cancellation in the last minute. Some of the trains are pretty new, some are the old ones. In general, trains are reliable. They are not very fast, comparing to buses /about 8 hours journey from Sofia to Varna/ but there are overnight trains with sleeping facilities where you can sleep comfortably while the train is carrying you to your destination. A place in a first class sleeping coach will cost you about 20 pounds per person. You can find destinations, timetables and prices at: www.razpisanie.bdz.bg.

When you get off the train or bus in Varna or Bourgas and need to go to a particular resort to the south or north, you can use the minibuses which will drive you from the Central bus or train station to your resort. They are cheap in comparison to taxis and run every 20 or 30 minutes. In case you prefer a taxi, you need to carefully check whether the taxi is legitimate or not. An illegal taxi can cost you a fortune.

Some people prefer hitch-hiking. Well, Bulgaria is not a dangerous place; hitch-hiking is relatively safe. The problem is that not many cars will stop to take a hitch-hiker. You can spend hours waving to cars before being picked up. I have done it in the past, it is fun and free, and you can try if you have time enough. Of course, hitch-hiking is not suitable for families with young children. As a tip, mainly the ordinary old cars would stop to pick up a hitch-hiker. The new luxurious cars, as a rule, would never stop, so do not waste your energy to wave at them.

WHERE AND WHAT TO EAT ON HOLIDAY IN BULGARIA?

In summer Bulgaria is paradise for vegetarians, vegans and veggie lovers. There are plenty of fresh vegetables and fruits which taste great. You can go to the local market and buy whatever you want. It is mainly local production, ripened under the sun. The prices at markets are lower than prices in the supermarkets or other shops. You will be usually allowed to try a piece of fruit or vegetable if you want, before buying. Actually, if a seller does not permit you to try, most probably his/her production is not very good or tasty. Do not insist; just go to the next salesman. If the price at some stalls is much higher than the others, it can mean that the fruits and vegetables are not locally produced but imported. Do not forget to wash your fruits or vegetables before eating them.

In the small resorts prices in supermarkets are higher than prices in the bigger towns. However, you can still shop in the small grocery stores; it would not cost a fortune to buy some food. You will be able to find many of your favorite English treats because they are imported especially for British tourists. However, you would not be able to find Irn-Bru in Bulgarian grocery stores. They have stopped selling Vanilla Coke as well.

In case you would like to eat in a restaurant, there is a huge choice in the resorts. Literally, there are restaurants at every corner, there are whole streets lined by restaurants. Do not get fooled by the luxurious appearance or shiny menus- follow the local people or follow the Bulgarian tourists. Usually, they would know where the best food is and where the best prices are. If a particular restaurant looks very pricey or luxurious it can mean that they are not able to sell their food as fast as they would like and need to process it again and put it in other dishes. In the cheap restaurants food is always fresh because it sells fast. If you see many Bulgarian people eating in a restaurant, you can sit there and eat with confidence. Usually waiting staff at restaurants speak or try to speak some English and you will be able to ask questions about food and ingredients. Do not forget to reveal the staff any allergies you may have. That can save you life because not all the ingredients will be written in the menu. Have a look at the menu- sometimes it can be fool of errors and can sound really funny. Avoid restaurants with errors in the menu. Those mistakes usually mean that the owner has been very greedy to pay 20 pounds to a professional translator to translate the menu in English. Instead, he had preferred to use Google translator. What can you expect from an owner who does not want to pay for professional translation? Good quality of food? Forget it; they will have the cheapest possible products and posh prices. You can find really good places to eat, with tasty dishes and good prices if you look around. Children are welcomed everywhere; restaurants usually provide special chairs for babies and toddlers. Most of the restaurants are dog friendly as well, as they do not want to lose any customers. Staff is friendly and waiters do usually speak foreign languages. Many restaurants are short of staff and you may be required to wait for your food for a longer time. On the streets you can buy pancakes, ice-cream, different types of take-away food if you prefer to eat in your room or just do not have desire to wait for food at a restaurant.

In most of the resorts there are English and Irish pubs as well, which provide English and Irish beer. Moreover, you will get the chance to watch English football matches there, on a big screen, surrounded by English fans. In the pubs beer and chips is the classic menu, however, you can also order fish, some other types of meat, meatballs, etc.

Try some traditional Bulgarian dishes- at first glance they may seem crazy, with weird combinations inside, as like as, yoghurt and cucumber cold soup. However, you may like them and find a whole new world of culinary delights. Vegetarian dishes are very popular in Bulgarian seasonal summer cuisine; they are prepared with peppers, cucumbers, tomatoes, eggplant, zucchini, etc. Big amounts of cheese are usually used in the traditional meals. Desserts are also delicious. Cakes are sweet and juicy; lots of desserts are prepared with seasonal fruits. Bulgarian desserts range from the simple to the elaborate and have been influenced by Greece, Turkey, Austria, and Germany. This reflects the different ethnic groups and culinary traditions that come together in Balkans. Nuts are often a part of Bulgarian desserts. You will often see crepes or pancakes offered for dessert in Bulgarian restaurants. These are served with sweet toppings or filled with chocolate pudding and whipped cream, honey or jam. Cakes are sweet and juicy; lots of desserts are prepared with seasonal fruits.

Of course, you should try Bulgarian wines, too. They are locally produced and have become famous around the world. Bulgaria exports wines to many countries, including the United Kingdom.

STRAY CATS AND DOGS

While you are eating in a restaurant, a non-expected visitor at your table may be a cat or a dog begging for food. In Bulgaria you can see stray dogs and cats everywhere on the streets. Unfortunately, there are no governmental policies related to abandoned pets. There are charities which are doing their best to help but they are usually small and do not have large funds. They do not receive money from governmental programs and count on volunteers and donations. You or your children may be tempted to pet the street cats and dogs. Well, cats are usually very friendly, they would not scratch nor bite, they will come to you meowing, looking for attention or food. If you carry with you a pack of cat food, all the cats around will come to eat. They allow to be petted; children would be safe in case they want to play with those cats. Dogs, on the reverse, sometimes can be dangerous. Not all stray dogs are dangerous, of course, but sometimes they tend to attack them, especially if they carry food. In general, cats are safe but avoid dogs in packs. You may even be tempted to adopt a stray cat or dog but it is recommendable to check regulations to see if it is possible /you can adopt it in Bulgaria, for sure, however, you need to check whether you are allowed to import it in the United Kingdom and what rules you need to follow/.

Travel To Bulgaria from Great Britain

MOSQUITOES AND OTHER INSECTS

You definitely will need a mosquito repellent if you want to spend your summer holiday in Bulgaria. **Mosquitoes** are everywhere; they really like the hot Bulgarian summer. The only place at the Bulgarian sea coast where I have never seen a single mosquito is the town of Sozopol. Perhaps its location makes that place unattractive for the blood sucking beasts- it is almost entirely surrounded by the sea. Probably the constant breezes take the mosquitoes away. Therefore, if your intention is to stay only in Sozopol, without moving around, you would be safe without using any repellents. Otherwise, it is obligatory to bring a repellent with you. The best and proven mosquito repellent is the AUTAN stick which is much better than AUTAN aerosol. I have tested many different types of mosquito repellents during my travelling around the world. In my opinion, the best choice is the AUTAN stick; it repels mosquitoes like a black magic. It is not expensive and you can find it in most of the Bulgarian pharmacies for the price of about 6 or 7 pounds. It is safe to be applied on children as well and smells well.

Wasps can be uninvited visitors of the beaches. They love food remnants and, because there are so many people eating and drinking on the beach, you can spot lots of wasps. Carefully choose your place at the beach- if the sand seems clean, without food or rubbish, you will probably not see any single wasp. Wasps also like water in hot weather and can be abundant around ponds, creeks, ditches, any water flow on the streets or even open water bottles. Be very careful and do not leave your bottles with water or fizzy drinks open- wasps can crawl inside and you can unintentionally drink them after that, which can be very dangerous- they can sting your tongue or throat. Their sting can cause allergy, therefore it is advisable to have anti-allergic pills.

Flies can be a real plague at some places. Flies also love rubbish and food scraps. They do not sting but bite like crazy and it can be very painful; they are not dangerous but can be very annoying. Try to close the door to the balcony whenever you go out, to keep the flies outside. Cover your food so that no flies land on it.

Cockroaches are some of the most disgusting and scary creatures you may see in your bathroom. In general, they are not very common to be spotted in the resorts; most probably you would see them during the night when you visit the bathroom. Light scares them and they will run away when you light the lamp. They are not dangerous, would not bite or sting you but they are scary.

MEDICAL HELP AND FIRST AID

You are required to have a valid medical insurance or a European Health Insurance Card in case you need medical help while on holiday abroad. In Bulgaria you can receive qualified medical services in any hospital or medical center, however, it is advisable to try to avoid the medical centers in the resorts- prices may be very expensive. In general, Bulgarian medical specialists are world-class specialists; therefore you can trust their advices. In Bulgaria you can still buy medicines without prescription from pharmacies, even antibiotics and mild anti-depressants. Pharmacists graduated universities and are fully qualified to advise you what medicines to buy.

CLIMATE CONDITIONS

Summers in Bulgaria are, in general, warm or hot. You can expect temperatures between 25ºC and 40ºC from June till mid-September. That is, actually, good news- you can save from luggage because you will not need to carry too many warm clothes. A waterproof jacket and sport shoes will be enough to protect you against any sudden weather changes. Leave at home your willies, warm jackets, long-sleeved shirts, etc. you will not need them. Take with you a pair of flip-flops or sandals, several T-shirts or short-sleeved shirts, shorts, a sun hat, and you will be prepared enough for summer conditions in Bulgaria. Do not forget your sun cream /you can also buy it in any Bulgarian supermarket or pharmacy/.

Winters may be very cold. Snow is common, especially in mountains, therefore, you have to prepare warm clothes- hats, scarfs, long warm trousers, winter jacket, warm socks and snow-proof boots. Thermal underwear will be a good idea. Remember that temperatures can fall below minus 20 degrees in January and February.

◆ ◆ ◆

CURRENCY EXCHANGE

Bulgarian currency is the Bulgarian lev. It has been bounded to the Euro for years and the value of two Bulgarian leva always equal to one Euro. Having in mind the current rate of the British pound against the Euro, one pound should be equal to about 2,10 Bulgarian leva. You must be careful when exchanging currency. In the resorts there are change bureaus which can give you extremely unprofitable rate of currency. Usually they also have huge commissions, written with very small print. The change bureaus have no obligation to stick to the official currency rates; therefore you can receive less money than expected. The banks are the best places to exchange foreign currency because they stick to the official rates. Do never try to exchange money on the street. There are many street dealers who will try to deceive the gullible tourists. The usual scheme used for ages is to give you a roll of paper, with only several real banknotes on the top. Do not trust the street dealers- they are very skilful and know lots of tricks. If you want to have a nice holiday and to still have money, run away from street dealers.

HOW TO BOOK ACCOMMODATION?

First, think about your preferences. How big is your family or the group of friends you will travel with? Would you need one room, two rooms, a studio, an apartment? Would you like breakfast to be included in the price? For example, if you like sleeping till late in the morning, breakfast will not be suitable for you, as it usually finishes by 10 a.m. However, if you are an early bird, a good breakfast would fuel you with energy for the rest of the day. Some accommodations offer dinner included in the price /good option for people who do not want to go to restaurants outside the hotel/ and some do provide full-board /suitable for organized people who can keep to the timetable/. Prices of accommodation can vary. The most luxurious places may cost hundreds of pounds per night per person and may include pampering like massages, spa, and hot tube in the price. Not necessarily the biggest price is related to the best place to stay. You can use online platforms like www.booking.com or www.trivago.com to find the most suitable place for you. It is worthy to read the reviews left by former costumers. Thus, you will be able to see what are the advantages and disadvantages of the particular accommodation. Location is very important. Be very careful and try to find before booking whether there is a noisy disco or bar next to the particular hotel.

If you want to spend a nice and relaxing holiday with your family, better avoid places with bars, pubs or discos in the near proximity. Although there is legislation related to the noise levels, no authority controls the observation of those laws and you can find yourself banging your head against the wall at 3 a.m., deprived of sleep because of the nearby disco. Cleanliness is also important, however, most of the hotels are clean and comfortable. Sometimes hot water can be a problem, especially in the seaside resorts, due to the thousands of tourists who shower at the same time.

In general, there can be water issues on the upper floors /8th, 9th and up/ of the hotels, therefore, it is recommendable to search for a room on the lower floors. Hotels and motels provide bed linen and towels, soap, shampoo toilet paper; therefore you will not be required to worry about those things. Towels are usually changed every day. You will have a small refrigerator and a TV in the room, studios provide household appliances and you will be able to cook your own food there. Tap water is drinkable, it is not necessary to buy bottled water every day. However, you may prefer the taste of the mineral bottled water which you can find in every shop.

I would recommend checking the smaller hotels, for example family hotels, guest houses, etc. Prices would be lower, the place would be cozier and, perhaps, friendlier, and usually huge breakfast is included in the price. Owners of those guest houses and family hotels really want to please the tourists and to provide them with a perfect stay, so you can have a really nice and relaxing holiday. Moreover, those family hotels often offer services like driving the tourists from the airport, early check-in, late check-out, excursions around, fishing trips, horse riding, etc. Read the descriptions and decide which will suit you.

In general, try to look for a hotel which is not situated on a noisy street, not very far from the beach /you would not really want to carry all your towels, bags, buckets, spades, etc. across the whole town/, preferably with a shop at walking distance. If you are in the mountain, the hotels situated next to the forest are the best and quietest. If you have children, it is essential to find a hotel with kids's facilities. Depending on the age of children, you may prefer a hotel with children's club and animation. Those clubs can be a real relief for overworked parents who need some time for relax. Many places provide playgrounds especially for children. As a rule, whenever there is a swimming-pool on the grounds of the hotel, there is a children's swimming-pool too.

PLACES TO STAY WHEN ON HOLIDAY IN BULGARIA

Bulgaria is a very popular destination for tourists from the United Kingdom and Northern Europe. In summer it is famous with its seaside resorts. The bankrupted tourist company Thomas Cook used to take many UK tourists to Sunny Beach in the summer. They had those all-inclusive packages which were filling in the hotels with British tourists. Sunny Beach was one of the best Bulgarian seaside resorts ten years ago but not anymore. Try to avoid Sunny Beach if you do not want to go to Bulgaria only because of the cheap alcohol. All kinds of alcohol are very cheap in Bulgaria. You can stay drunk during the whole holiday and still have some money when you come back to England. A big bottle of beer /2 liters/ costs only a pound and a bottle of vodka /0.75 liters/ can vary in price from as less as 4 pounds / not very good quality, though/ to 15 pounds. Unfortunately, cheap prices have been attracting for years tourists whose only desire is to get drunk and to stay drunk. The fame of Sunny Beach is of a place where you can get drunk, crawl the bars and the pubs, have alcohol tours, and stay drunk till you fly back home. Nowadays this resort is very popular among young people, those who are travelling for the first time abroad without parents. The pubs, bars and discos in Sunny Beach are open 24 hours a day, hotels offer relatively cheap all-inclusive packs and young people can have endless fun. Unfortunately, that is not a place where families or couples, or parents would like to go. If you want to enjoy your holiday, try to avoid Sunny Beach. Instead, you can head to the North or to the South. Both directions have their advantages and disadvantages.

If you decide to go to the North, you can stay in the city of Varna. Varna is the third largest city in Bulgaria and the largest one on the Black Sea shore. Because of its history and its economical and cultural significance, it is often called the Sea Capital of Bulgaria. The town was founded in the remote past, in the 6th century BC under the name of Odessos. Nowadays Varna is very popular among tourists because of its cultural, archeological and tourist attractions. If you go to Varna, you can enjoy the Sea Garden of Varna which offers multiple entertainment options – there is a Roman amphitheater, an astronomical complex, an observatory, a planetarium and a tower on its territory, as well as multiple entertainment platforms and a small rowing channel for children, a pool for water wheels and a zoo. You can see there remains of the ancient civilizations in the territory of Bulgaria. Being a crossroad for centuries, it became a meeting point of many nations and tribes. In fact, nobody can answer the questions arising from the discovery of the ancient gold treasure. Its origin is still unknown, as well as the civilization which created it. You can spend hours in the archeological Museum of Varna; it is definitely a place to remember. There is also the Dolphinarium where you can enjoy the spectacle of dolphins. The beaches of Varna are sandy, large and relatively clean. One very famous attraction is the water-slide- it is cheap, safe and there is a lifeguard beside the pool. Children really enjoy the water-slide, as like as the adults.

Due to the fact that Varna is not a resort but a functioning town, the restaurants, pubs, bars and other places are not expensive. A family of four can eat and drink for 20 pounds at a restaurant. You can buy food on the street or take-away for as less as 2 pounds. The restaurants and dining establishments are clean and the food is of good quality. If you want to eat sea food, please, remember that most of the sea food has been imported from Greece or Spain. Although Bulgaria is a country with a long sea shore, the fishing industry is not very developed. The paradox is that the fish caught in the Black Sea can be more expensive than the imported fish.

To the North of Varna there are several nice small towns, where tourists can relax and have fun. A very famous town is Kavarna. For more than ten years the most famous heavy metal and rock bands were playing in Kavarna and made it the "Rock capital of the Balkans". The rock and heavy metal fans will be amazed by the monument of Dio in the center of the town and the murals on the walls of the high blocks of flats, depicting different rock and heavy metal musicians. Currently, Kavarna is a small town, the central beach is of poor quality, however, nearby is one of the most beautiful beaches in Europe, called "Bolata". Near Kavarna is situated the Cape of Kaliakra and the Kaliakra nature reserve, where dolphins and cormorants can be observed. If you visit Kaliakra, you will not be left disappointed, for sure.

If you do not like overcrowded places and want to escape the hectic life of the cities, I would recommend you to head to the North. You can find good accommodation opportunities in Shabla which is the last Bulgarian town before the Romanian border. It is a small town with beautiful beaches. The lack of crowds has turned it into a preferred resort for people who want to relax or just escape from the everyday life. Before going to Shabla, you may like to visit the Botanical Garden of Balchik where you can see plants from all over the world.

There also are two famous resorts on the Northern coast - Golden Sands and Albena. Both are still family friendly and much quieter and suitable for relax than Sunny Beach.

Northern Bulgarian seacoast is more rocky and steeper than the Southern. It is less populated and you can find some nature retreats to relax.

If you decide to go to the South, you will discover the beautiful small towns of Sozopol, Nessebar, Primorsko, Kiten, Saint Vlas, etc. Sozopol and Nessebar are the oldest towns on the Bulgarian sea coast. Both were established by the ancient Greeks and you will really enjoy their old architecture, ancient remains, medieval churches, and the sense of history. One of my favourite places in sozopol is the Archeological museum. It is located in the old part of the town. The Archaeological Museum reveals the history and the millennial cultural traditions of the town of Sozopol from the end of the 6th millennium BC to the 17th century AD. Visitors of the Archaeological Museum can see the alabaster casket containing for centuries the relics of John the Baptist and a small box with a Greek inscription talking about the journey of the relics to St. Ivan Island. I would recommend about 2 hours for most visitors. Sozopol is surrounded by the sea and, as I mentioned already above, there are no mosquitoes. The other place of interest for people who enjoy history and archeology is Nessebar. The old and the new town of Nessebar are connected via a narrow man-made isthmus. nessebar is rich of old churches, ancient remains, old houses. The whole town is full of history. In addition to this, the modern part of the town provides many hotels, guest houses, family hotels for tourists.

To the South you can visit the small resorts of Kiten, Primorsko, Tzarevo, Sinemoretz. They are family friendly and popular for their low prices and good service.

You can combine your holiday in Bulgaria with a holiday in Greece or Turkey. Bulgaria has a long border with Greece to the south, both are European Union member-states; therefore it is easy to travel to both countries. There are many border checkpoints, usually there are no cues of cars and no additional documents are required. As a tourist you will drive either your own car, or a rented vehicle. If you are driving your own car, you would have your Green card insurance already done. In case you rent a car and would like to visit Greece, you need to make Green card insurance, in addition to the required third-party liability insurance. Do not forget that it is against the law to drive in flip-flops in Greece. You can get a huge fine for such traffic offence.

In case you have chosen to spend your summer holiday in Bulgarian mountains /Rhodope Mountain, Rila or Pirin/, you can travel very easy to the Greek Mediterranean beaches. After driving for just few hours, you can reach the beautiful Greek seaside, passing through one of the many border checkpoints between Bulgaria and Greece. For example, if you go through the Makaza pass, you will reach the Greek towns of Kavala and Komotini or the village of Keramoti in just two hours of driving. From Keramoti you can take the ferry to the island of Thasos.

In general, you will make a good choice if you decide to spend a part of your summer holiday in the Bulgarian mountains. There are some very popular ski resorts which are full in winter but deserted in summer. Therefore, prices are much cheaper; service is as good as in winter, there is more space for tourists and no cues for the attractions.

Climate conditions in the mountains are usually steady. Weather in summer is warm during the day and colder during the night. You will need a jacket, long trousers and shoes for the cold nights and sun hat and sun cream during the day.

Bulgarian mountains are really beautiful, with green forests, wild animals /if you are lucky, you can see deer, rabbits, and wild boars. You can see traces from bears, wolves and other big animals. Ski lifts work in summer and will take you to the peaks from where you will be able to look around and to see the whole beauty of the mountain. I would recommend checking the resorts of Pamporovo, Chepelare, Smolyan for accommodation. In summer you can ride horses in the mountains /suitable for beginners and advanced riders/. You can even go fishing in a lake or a dam. The owners of the hotel or the guest house would usually provide you with everything you need to fish. Fishing is a very relaxing experience- in the heart of the nature; surrounded by silence you will be able to switch off and to forget the everyday worries. You can also visit some caves. For example, Yagodinska Cave is famous for its Eneolithic dwellings. Yagodinska cave is located 20 km south of Devin. Some very beautiful cave formations can be seen along the entire tourist route – stalactites, stalagmites, columns, helictites, cave lakes, dendrites and some of the most unique formations – cave pearls. In the cave there even is a ritual hall for civil marriages. Another interesting cave is the Magura Cave, which is situated in the North-Western part of Bulgaria, not very far from the town of Belogradchik. It is famous for its cave paintings, made about 10 000 years ago.

Another very popular tourist place, famous for its mineral waters and spa, is the town of Velingrad. Forests around are wonderful for walking, you can also ride horses in the mountain. Not very far from Velingrad is situated the village of Dorkovo where you will have the unique opportunity to visit the paleontological park with museum. You will see skeletons and bones of the huge animal species which inhabited this region in the remote past- mammoths, rhinos, antelopes, deer, and three-toed horses.

If you have time and are interested in history, I would recommend visiting the Old Bulgarian capital of Veliko Tarnovo. It is situated in the mountain of Stara Planina, in the middle of the distance between Sofia and Varna. The castle and the fortress are amazing and in the night there is a light and sound show.

ENJOY YOUR JOURNEY TO BULGARIA

The most important advice should say: "Enjoy your journey to Bulgaria". It is a country you would like to visit again because you will fall in love with its beautiful nature, sandy beaches and green mountains. Life is relatively cheap, people are friendly, many people speak English /or try to speak/, sun will never betray you /most of the summer days are sunny and warm/, there are many places of interest to be seen and many attractions suitable for kids and adults.

Printed in Great Britain
by Amazon